28 AMERICAN ART SONGS

for High Voice and Piano

ISBN 978-1-4950-0070-6

G. SCHIRMER, *Inc.*

DISTRIBUTED BY

HAL•LEONARD®
CORPORATION

7777 W. BLUEMOUND RD. P.O. BOX 13819 MILWAUKEE, WI 53213

www.musicsalesclassical.com
www.halleonard.com

CONTENTS

It's all I have to bring

Emily Dickinson*

Ernst Bacon

*Words printed by special permission.

The Crucifixion
from *Hermit Songs*

From The Speckled Book, 12th Century
Translated by Howard Mumford Jones

Samuel Barber
Op. 29, No. 5

Text from *Romanesque Lyric*, by permission of the University of North Carolina Press.

Ah, sore was the suff-'ring borne By the bod-y of Ma-ry's Son, But sor-er still to Him was the grief Which for His sake Came up-on His Moth - er.

Oct. 26, 1952

The Daisies

James Stephens

Samuel Barber
Op. 2, No. 1

Poem from *Collected Poems of James Stephens*. Printed by permission of The Macmillan Company, publishers.

wan- dered hap- p'ly,* to and fro; I kissed my dear on ei - ther cheek, In the bud of the morn - ing— O. A lark sang up from the breez - y land, A lark sang down from a cloud a - far, As she and I went hand in hand In the field where the dais - ies are.

The Windmill,
Rogers Park
July 20, 1927

*In Stephens' poem the word is "happily," which Barber chose to set on two notes rather than three.

Hey nonny no!

from *Three Songs: The Words from Old England*

Anonymous (16th century)

Samuel Barber

With boisterous good-humor!

Hey non-ny no! Hey non-ny no! Men are fools that wish to

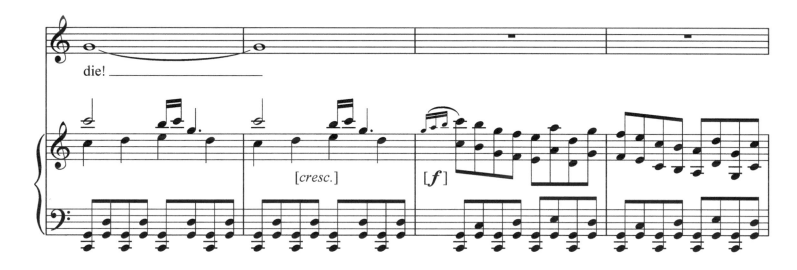

die!

Is't not fine to dance and sing When the bells of death do ring?

There are no dynamics in Barber's manuscript; minimal suggestions have been made.

To Isabelle Vengerova
The Monk and His Cat
from *Hermit Songs*

8th or 9th century
Translated by W.H. Auden

Samuel Barber
Op. 29, No. 8

Words used by special permission.

*Notes marked (–) in these two measures should be slightly longer, pochissimo rubato; also on the fourth page. [Barber's footnote]

I re-joice when my mind Fath-oms a prob-lem.

Pleased with his own art, ___ Neith-er hin-ders the oth-er;

___ Thus we live e - ver ___ With-out te-dium and en - vy.

Pan-gur, white Pan - gur, ___

How — hap - py — we are — A - lone to - geth-er, — Scho - lar and cat. —

Pan-gur, white Pan - gur, —

How — hap - py — we are. —

Feb. 16, 1953

A Slumber Song of the Madonna

Alfred Noyes

Samuel Barber

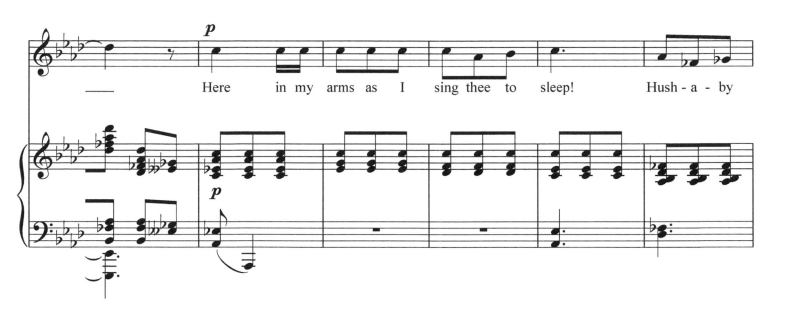

Here in my arms as I sing thee to sleep! Hush - a - by

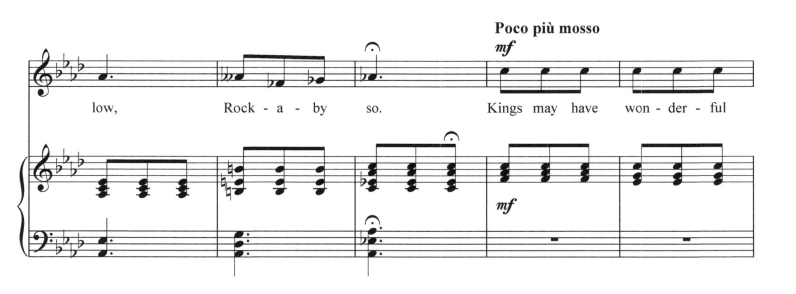

Poco più mosso

low, Rock - a - by so. Kings may have won - der - ful

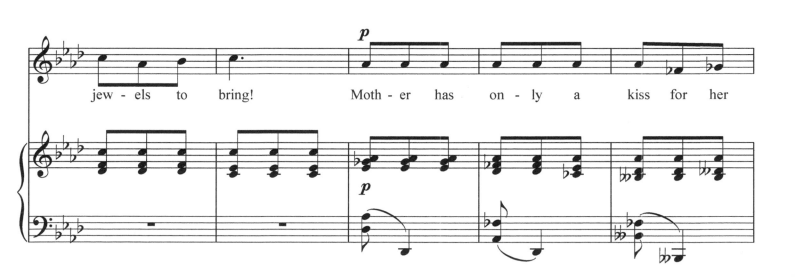

jew - els to bring! Moth - er has on - ly a kiss for her

cresc. poco a poco

king. Why should my sing - ing So make me to weep?

On - ly I know that I love thee, I love thee!

Tempo primo

Love thee, my lit - tle one, _____ Sleep!

Mother, I cannot mind my wheel

Walter Savage Landor

Samuel Barber

men may use de - ceit;

[mf] [dim.] [poco rit.]
He al - ways said my eyes _____ were

[cresc.]

blue, And of - ten swore my lips _____ were

[a tempo]
[p]
sweet. _____

[a tempo] [p] [poco rit.]

To Sara

Sure on this shining night

James Agee

Samuel Barber
Op. 13, No. 3

Text from *Permit Me Voyage*. Used by permission of Yale University Press, Publishers.

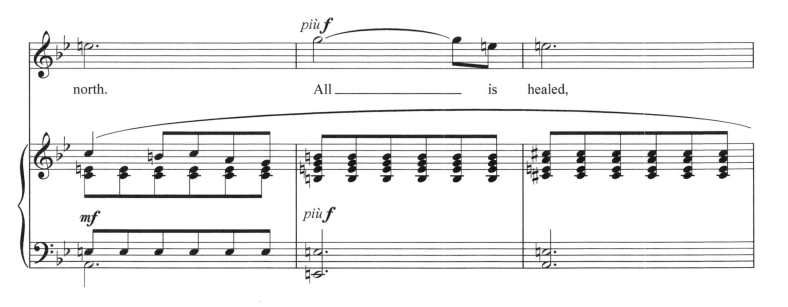

north. All _____ is healed,

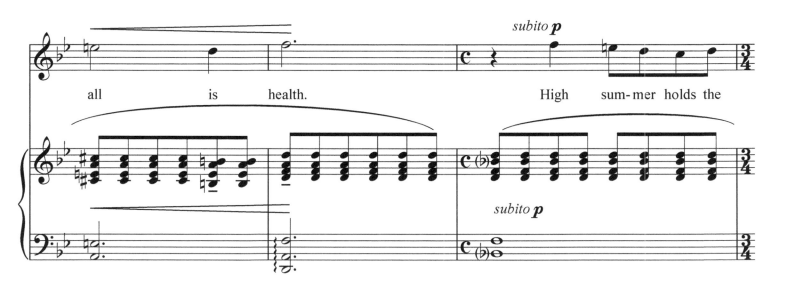

all is health. High sum-mer holds the

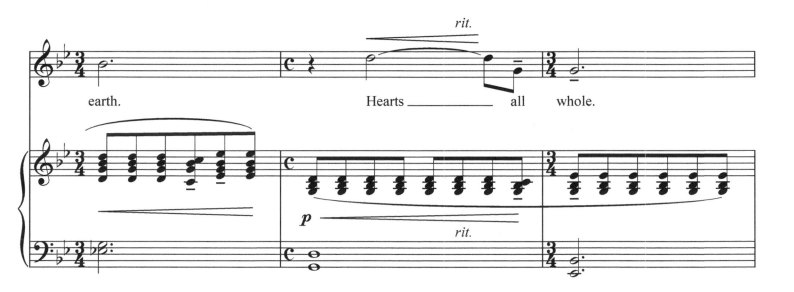

earth. Hearts _____ all whole.

Sure on this shin-ing night I weep for won - der

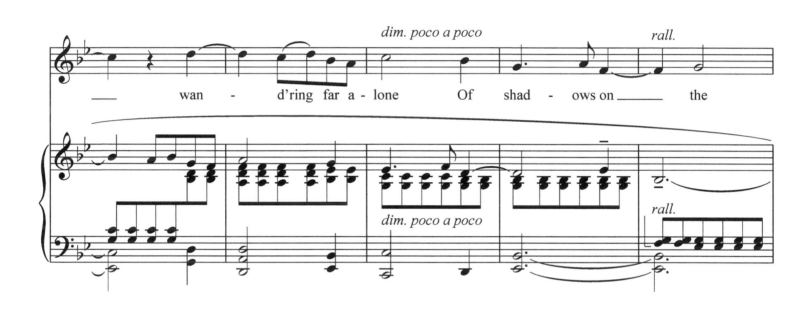

wan - d'ring far a - lone Of shad - ows on the

stars.

September 1938

Heavenly Grass

Tennessee Williams

Paul Bowles

feet took a walk   In   heav - en - ly grass.   All   night while the lone - some

stars   rolled past,   Then my   feet come down   to   walk   on   earth   And my

moth - er cried When she   give   me birth.

Now my feet walk_ far And my feet walk fast, But they still got an itch for_ heav-en-ly grass. But they still got an itch for_ heav'n-ly grass._____

Cabin

Tennessee Williams

Paul Bowles

Sugar in the Cane

Tennessee Williams

Paul Bowles

ba - ker. ____ I'm sweet sug - ar in the cane, ___

Nev - er touched ex - cept by rain. ____

If you touched me God save you, These sum - mer days are hot and

blue. ____

I'm po - ta - toes not yet mashed, I'm a check that ain't been

cashed. _____ I'm a win - dow with a blind, _

Can't see what goes on be - hind. _____

If you did, God save your soul! These win - ter nights are blue and

cold! _____

ten.

8vb

To Sophie Sargent

The Lamb

William Blake

Theodore Chanler

When I Have Sung My Songs

Words and Music by
Ernest Charles

To Lawrence Tibbett

Loveliest of Trees

A. E. Housman*

John Duke

*Poem from "A Shropshire Lad." Printed by permission of Grant Richards, London, publisher.

And take from sev - en - ty springs a score, It on - ly leaves me fif - - - ty more.

To George Hamlin

Do not go, my love

Words by
Sir Rabindranath Tagore

Music by
Richard Hageman

to the Guide

Where the Music Comes From

Words and Music by
Lee Hoiby

I want to be where the mu-sic comes from, Where the clock stops, where it's now. I want to be with the friends a-round me Who have found me, who show me

how. I want to sing to the ear - ly morn - ing, See the

sun - light melt the snow; And oh, _____ I want to

grow. _____

I want to

*pronounced *day – vas* (nature spirits)

Serenity

John Greenleaf Whittier
(from *The Brewing of Soma*)

Charles Ives
(adapted 1919)

In the mornin'

Negro spiritual (before 1850) communicated
to Ives in 1929 by Mary Evelyn Stiles

Accompaniment by
Charles Ives

To Mme. Povla Frijsh

The Pasture

Robert Frost*

Charles Naginski

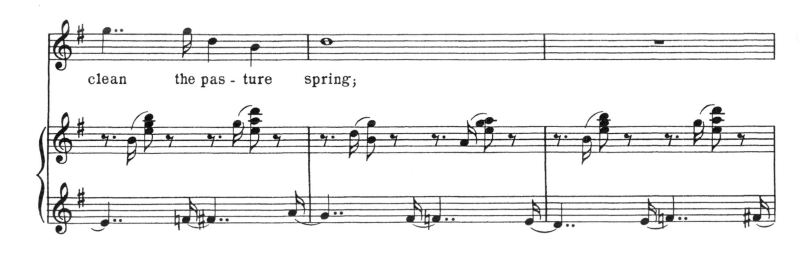

*From "Collected Poems" by Robert Frost. By permission of Henry Holt and Company, Publishers.

wait   to watch the   wa - ter   clear,_____   I   may):

I   sha'nt be gone   long.—   You   come too.

I'm go-ing out   to   fetch   the lit - tle   calf   That's stand-ing   by   the

moth - er. It's so young, It tot-ters when she

licks it with her tongue.

I sha'n't be gone long.— You come too.

To Miriam Witkin

The Green Dog

Words and Music by
Herbert Kingsley

Black is the color of my true love's hair

Text collected and adapted by
John Jacob Niles
Music by John Jacob Niles

love ___ the grass where - on she stands.

I ___ love my_love and_ well she knows, I

love _____ the grass where-on she goes; If __ she on _ earth no __

more__ I __ see, My life____ will quick-ly leave me.

mp

I__ go to_Troub-le-some* to mourn, to weep, But

sat - is-fied I ne'er can sleep; I'll__ write her a note in__

a few lit - tle lines, I'll suf - fer death ten thou-sand times.

*Troublesome Creek, which empties into the Kentucky River.

Black, black, black is the col-or of my true love's hair, Her lips _____ are some-thing ro - sy fair, The__ pert - est_ face and the dain - ti -est_ hands— I love_____ the grass where-on she stands.

Go 'way from my window

Words and Music by
John Jacob Niles
Arranged by the composer

both- er me no__ more._____ I'll
long as song - birds sing._____ I'll
on ac- count of__ you._____ Go
real- ly did love best._____ Go 'way__ from my win-dow, Go

'way__ from my door, Go 'way, 'way, 'way from my bed - side And

rit. e dim.

both- er me no more,__ And both- er me no__ more.

The Lass from the Low Countree

Text adapted by J.J.N.

Music by
John Jacob Niles

milk-white steed; _____ She smil-ed and she spoke, but he paid no heed., Oh,

sor - row, sing sor - row! Now she sleeps in the val - ley where the

wild - flow-ers nod, And no one knows she loved him but her - self and God; _____

If you be a lass from the Low Coun-tree, Don't

8 - ♩

To Helen-Claire Moyle

American Lullaby

Words and Music by
Gladys Rich

Hush-a - bye, you sweet lit-tle ba - by, And don't you cry__ an-y

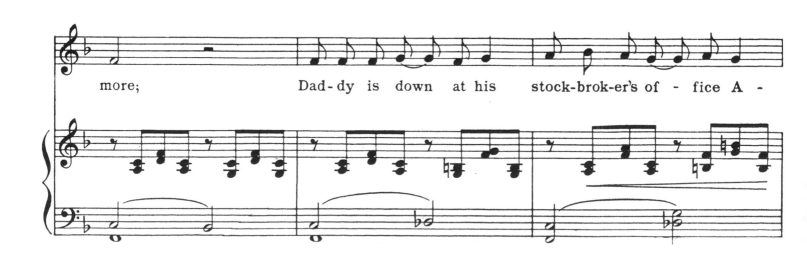

more; Dad-dy is down at his stock-brok-er's of - fice A -

keep-ing the wolf__ from the door.

Nurs-ie will raise the win-dow shade high, So you can see__ the

poco accel. *a tempo*

cars whiz-zing by.__ Home in a hur - ry each Dad-dy must fly__ To a

ba - by   like   you.

Hush - a - bye,   you   sweet lit - tle   ba - by,   And

close those   pret - ty blue   eyes.   Moth-er has gone to her

week-ly bridge par - ty To   get her wee ba - by the   prize.

For Giuseppe De Luca

This Little Rose

Emily Dickinson*

William Roy

*Poem copyright © 1945, by Millicent Todd Bingham.

thee.

slightly accelerated - - - - -

mp

p

On-ly a bee will miss it, On-ly a but-ter - fly,

p

Hast-en-ing from far jour - ney On— its breast to lie.

slightly accelerated - - - - -

mp cresc.

slightly ac -

mf

Holiday Song

Genevieve Taggard*

William Schuman
Arranged by the composer

When was it ev - er a

waste of time to climb ___ hills? When was it ev - er a

use - less thing to sing the song of a long jol - ly day in the sun?

*Words printed by exclusive permission.

bout, to sing and shout, to sing and shout, shout!

8vb

Tempo II circa 160

Lo! Dee-de-lee dee, dee-de-lee dee,

8vb

Lo! Dee-de-lee dee, dee-de-lee dee, dee-de-lee dee.

p

Dee - a, dee - a, dee - a, dee - a, Lo!

8va

8va

Ped. *

New Rochelle, N.Y.
May 26, 1942
Arranged for solo
voice May, 1946

Orpheus with his lute

William Shakespeare
(From "Henry VIII")

William Schuman

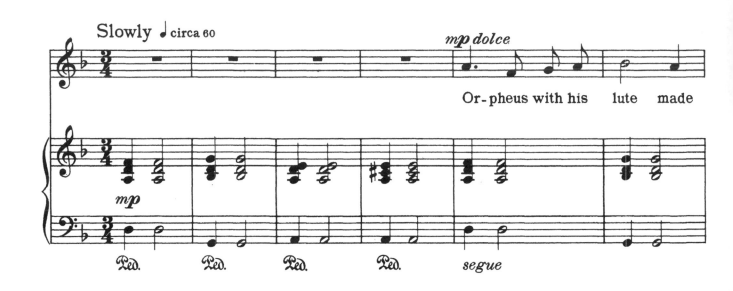

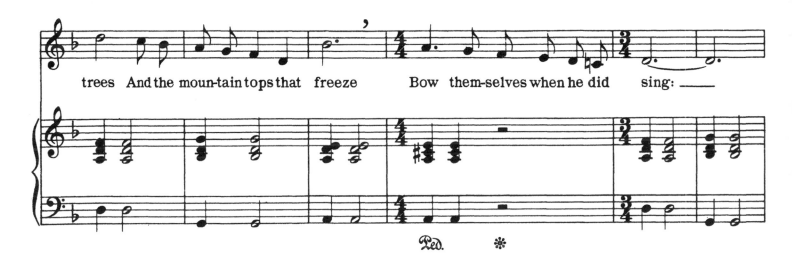

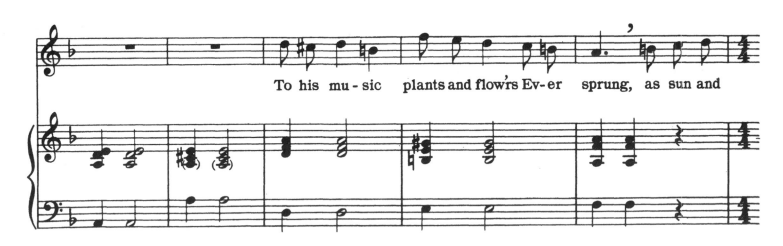

show'rs There had made a last-ing spring._____ Ev-'ry thing that heard him

play, E-ven the bil-lows of the sea, Hung their heads, and then lay

by._____ In sweet mu-sic is such art, Kill-ing care and grief of

heart, Fall a-sleep, or hear-ing, die._____

New Rochelle, N.Y.
August 6, 1944

Brother Will, Brother John

Elizabeth Charles Welborn

John Sacco

With sly jocularity ♩ = 82

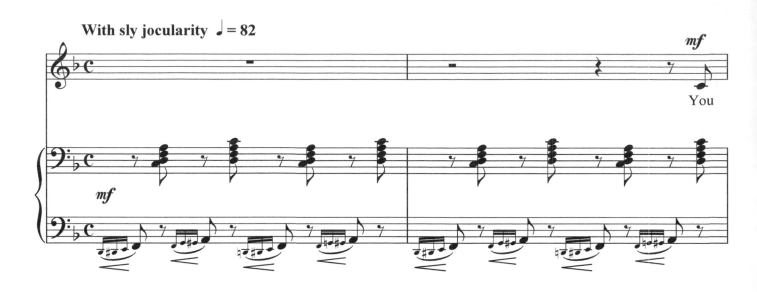

ain't no use, Mis - ter, af - ter you're gone, ___ You

can't take it with you, Broth - er Will, Broth - er John.

sly, provocative

Shake a leg here, shake a leg there,

laugh a lit - tle, smile a lit - tle, spread a lit - tle cheer, Broth - er